MOTORCYCLE MANIA

MOTORCYCLE MANIA

The publishers would like to thank the following sources for their kind permission to
reproduce the pictures in this book:

Kel Edge; David Goldman; London Features/J. Burstein, Geoff De Guire, Scott Donie,
David Fisher, Phil Loftus, Kevin Maxur, Ilpo Musto, Derek Ridgers; Phil Masters;
Don Morley; Pictorial Press/Andrew Morland; Rex Features/Richard Foreman, David Taylor,
Bill Tinney, Richard Young; Garry Stuart.

Every effort has been made to acknowledge correctly and contact the source and/or
copyright holder of each picture, and Carlton Books Limited apologises for any
unintentional errors or omissions which will be corrected in future editions of this book.

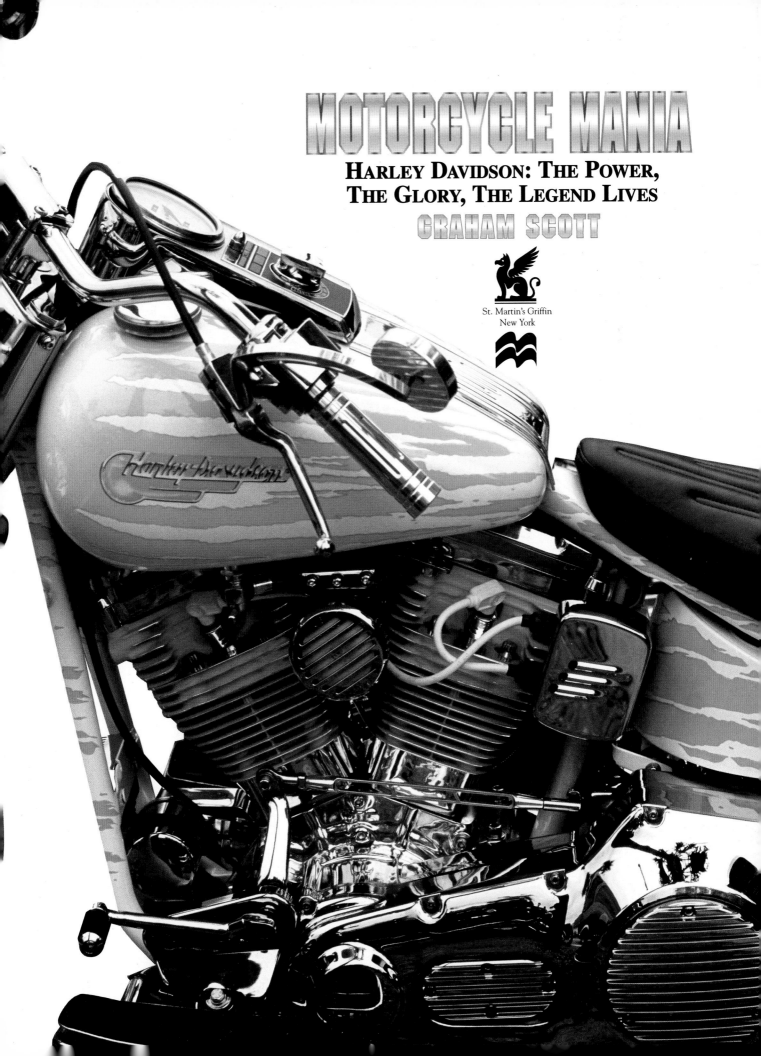

MOTORCYCLE MANIA

HARLEY DAVIDSON: THE POWER, THE GLORY, THE LEGEND LIVES

GRAHAM SCOTT

St. Martin's Griffin
New York

THE CONTENTS

MOTORCYCLE MANIA

The Harley-Davidson story is different to a tale about virtually any other vehicle or make. Perhaps the only possible parallels to the owners of Harley-Davidsons are the "Tifosi," the Italian fans of Ferrari, or the "Ducatisti," who venerate the Ducatis. The Harley's story is not simply a tale of machinery, racing success and business booms and busts. It is certainly a richer tale than that of a company that makes motorbikes and has done for a long time.

THE SLOGAN RAN "YOU MEET THE NICEST PEOPLE ON A HONDA," BUT SOMEHOW THE SAME PHRASE DOESN'T QUITE TRANSLATE TO HARLEY-DAVIDSONS.

Sure, Harley-Davidson makes motorbikes, it has had racing success and would appear to be on a return to those great days, but this is more about the effect the bikes have had on the lives of millions of people, from paupers to presidents.

For a worn-out factory worker, his old Shovelhead is the one extravagance of his life, it is a statement that says he is still an individual. For the Hell's Angel his Knucklehead is his most trusted companion, a bike that is as much a part of him as the colors he wears on his back. For the successful executive it is a bit of escapism, his Dyna Low Rider the perfect mount for getting out there at the end of the week to put some cruising miles between him and reality. And for the middle-aged couple, their old Electra Glide is still the only way to go touring and see their God-given country.

For years such people have been badly served by the company they have remained faithful to, but in the last decade or so the tide has changed. The company is confident, active and trying out new ideas. You know it is doing something right because the Japanese have been copying the big

Milwaukee monsters for years now, trying to replicate something you just can't fake.

The Evolution engine has been part of the revolution, a modern engine on the classic lines; but the company is not just slavishly copying the past. You might get that impression from looking at the bikes with Springer forks and Softail rear end, styling mimicking past models, but this same company is now developing a V-twin with electronic fuel injection, liquid cooling, DOHC and four valves per cylinder.

Harley-Davidson has a future, more secure than it has been for a long time, and that is mainly because the faith of millions of people has finally proven to be well-founded. In return the company will now look after you. The most American of companies is now thinking almost like the communists used to, with a program that will watch over you almost from the cradle to the grave.

The big V-twins can now be bought with a bewildering array of models and letters, but it really means you can get exactly what you want, and if you can't the company's after-market tuning and accessory packages will help you there too.

You can buy clothing and virtually anything you can think of that could take the coveted Harley-Davidson logo; everything from a pen to earrings and a beach towel. Harley-Davidson can now be with you all the time, not just when you're on your bike. You can ride it, wear it, drink from it, watch it—a steadying and reliable force in your entire life.

May that force be with you.

THIS SPORTSTER FROM THE 1970S DISPLAYS NOT MUCH TASTE BUT A LOT OF TIME SPENT WITH ALCOHOL AND AN ENGRAVING TOOL.

IN THE BEGINNING

We are nearly at the end of a century and Harley-Davidsons have been around since the beginning of it. It was in 1903—the same year that the Wright brothers managed a series of hops in their biplane, "Flyer I"— that the first production Harley-Davidson was made.

IN THE BEGINNING

In 1909, the same year that Frenchman Louis Bleriot flew across the English Channel in his 25bhp monoplane, the first V-twin Harley appeared. Now, as the end of the century appears, we have flown faster than sound and landed men on the moon. And we still ride Harley-Davidson V-twins. The story is in many ways a classic tale of American ingenuity and willpower eventually backed up by engineering might. However, it also starts as a typical tale of a newly-formed country, a melting pot of talent and ideas. Two young engineers, friends since childhood, decided to try to make a motorized bicycle. William Harley and Arthur Davidson worked on

it in their spare time and soon drew in Arthur's brother, Walter. Their brother William Davidson, a skilled tool-maker also joined the group, but they wouldn't have moved as far as fast if it hadn't been for a German immigrant who knew enough about the French de Dion engine design to make some basic working diagrams.

The American/French/German concoction worked, but you can look in vain in the official history books on Harley-Davidson for the identity of the German engineer.

The four men made three single-cylinder, three-horsepower bikes in 1903 and three more the following year. On their wooden shed door this qualified them to proudly paint "Harley-Davidson Motor Co." They were in business.

EARLY SINGLE SHOWS IN CLOSE-UP HOW THE APPEARANCE OF THE ENGINE WAS IMPROVED BY THE MECHANICALLY DRIVEN INLET VALVES, INTRODUCED IN 1911.

A FACTORY RACER FROM THE EARLY 1920S FEATURES THE 74CU IN V-TWIN, A POTENT MIX ON THE BOARD RACE-TRACKS.

Bill Harley, the engineer of the group, went on to study combustion engine design, work which bore fruit when he designed the first V-twin around 1909, effectively grafting two of the single-cylinder engines together at 45 degrees. Early successes were a combination of sales acumen—they had a dealer network in place by 1910—and a reputation built on making strong machines. The very first bike they made covered over 100,000 miles by 1913 and was still running on its original major components. When you think of the engineering knowledge available then, that is quite an achievement.

By the 1920s the company's reputation was further enhanced by a vigorous racing program, the Wrecking Crew in particular showing that Harleys were tough bikes that could take on anyone, anywhere. Racing speeded up the engineering, with twin cams appearing on bikes as early as 1920,

EARLY V-TWINS WERE BASICALLY JUST TWO SINGLE CYLINDERS GRAFTED TOGETHER AT AN ANGLE OF 45 DEGREES, BUT INVESTMENT IN METALLURGY MEANT THEY PROVED RELIABLE.

and of course the engines grew in size to match the demand for more power. The first 74cu in (cubic inch, equivalent to 1200cc) engine in the JD came out in 1921, an engine size that was to run right through to the present day. The number of specifications, sizes and ideas that have come down to us in the present day unchanged from more than 70 years ago is extraordinary.

By the end of the First World War the factory was a large brick building in Juneau Avenue, Milwaukee, and by the Second World War Harley-Davidsons

VERY EARLY SINGLE CYLINDER, AROUND 1910, DISPLAYS THE SPRINGER FORKS DEVELOPED BY BILL HARLEY AND THE ENORMOUS BELT DRIVE TO THE REAR WHEEL.

were supporting troops all over the planet, the WLA 45cu in V-twin being a dependable tool to men in need. As you can read in Chapter Three, disenchanted ex-servicemen came back to Harley-Davidsons after the war, the bikes continuing to play a central role in their lives.

By now the company had produced its first overhead-valve V-twin, the Knucklehead coming out in 1936. The 74cu in Knucklehead, came out five years later, a better memory of the year than Pearl Harbor. Four years after the Second World War ended saw the springer front-ends being replaced on some models by hydraulic suspension. The 61cu in Panhead got the soft ride first, with others soon following.

The late 1950s saw a burst of energy at opposite ends of the spectrum with the FLH 74cu in tourers coming out as well as the first Sportster, a 55cu in overhead-valve model, with rear suspension appearing on the Duo Glide and the first hydraulic brake. But 1965 was one of the biggest years

TOP

HARLEY-DAVIDSONS HAVE HAD SIDECARS ATTACHED TO THEM SINCE 1914—A USEFUL ACCESSORY WHEN YOU ONLY HAVE A SINGLE SADDLE.

because it saw the arrival of the Electra Glide, another of those seminal Harleys that continues to this day. The models were coming but all was not well. The America of the Vietnam War was a nervous time of mergers and acquisitions, and Harley-Davidson had some major predators circling it.

THE 74CU IN VL WAS FIRST INTRODUCED IN 1930 AND RAN INTO LOADS OF PROBLEMS, BUT BY THE TIME PRODUCTION STOPPED IN 1940 IT WAS A DEPENDABLE, FAIRLY POWERFUL BIKE.

RIGHT ▶

THE EXTREMELY ELEGANT 1939 KNUCKLEHEAD EL. THIS 61CU IN V-TWIN HAD A FEW TEETHING PROBLEMS WITH LUBRICATION WHEN INTRODUCED IN 1936 BUT THIS WAS SOON DEALT WITH.

◀ **LEFT**

TOP THE MILITARY PLAYED SUCH A BIG PART IN SALES THAT EVEN CIVILIAN BIKES CAME IN KHAKI GREEN—THIS IS A 45CU IN WLC WITHOUT SCREEN AND PANNIERS, FOR USE BY THE CANADIAN ARMY.

EARLY IRON-HEAD 55CU IN XL SPORTSTER, THE START OF A DESIGN THAT IS NOW THE ENTRY VEHICLE TO THE HARLEY-DAVIDSON RANGE.

RIGHT

In 1968 the shareholders voted to merge with American Machine & Foundry (AMF) rather than risk being taken over by a more aggressive company. Early leaders left, often making a nice profit on their shares, and the company changed, often for the better with more modern management practices and a massive, sustained injection of investment.

A tie-up with the Italian Aermacchi company brought in cheaper bikes with the Harley-Davidson name on the tank, but who believed the two-stroke road and dirt

bikes were really Harleys? At the same time, bikes like the Super Glide continued the more honored tradition—so long as they were well put together.

Overall, the 1970s were a mess, with the aftermath of the Vietnam War, pollution legislation, the Oil Crisis and intense pressure from the Japanese. This was made worse when charges that the Japanese were "dumping" bikes on the U.S. market were not fully substantiated. AMF started to lose some will and direction and a dozen men decided to buy Harley-Davidson back. All they had to do was raise about $75 million.

Incredibly, they did it, and the event that has gone down in H-D legend as a red letter, upper-

BELOW ▼ A 1970s XLCR SPORTSTER AFTER IT HAS BEEN TYPICALLY ALTERED BY A SERIES OF OWNERS. NO TWO HARLEYS ARE EVER ALIKE.

MAIN & INSET

A TYPICAL CUSTOMER CUSTOM, A FAT BOY WITH STRAIGHT PIPES BUT THE DISTINCTIVE SOLID DISHED WHEELS. EVOLUTION ENGINE STOPS THE OIL MIXING WITH THE SEA WATER.

A 1340CC SOFTAIL CUSTOM TAKES THE STRAIN ON DAYTONA BEACH. THE DESIGN LOOKS LIKE A HARDTAIL BUT REAR SUSPENSION IS TUCKED UP OUT OF SIGHT.

 THIS MODERN ELECTRA GLIDE CLASSIC IS NOT QUITE THE TOP OF THE RANGE BUT YOU GET SOME IDEA OF THE CARRYING CAPACITY AND COMFORT AVAILABLE.

case event, The Buyback happened in 1981. It was move that shocked some people, and thrilled millions. AMF saw Harley-Davidson more as an industrial plant rather than a consumer-provider, and now we can see, with the benefit of hindsight, that the way forward for any motorcycle manufacturer is as a provider of leisure pursuit machinery.

Since The Buyback, the company has moved on steadily, most notably in 1983 when it unveiled the completely new Evolution range of engines,

modern, oil-tight and reliable and the cylinders still at 45 degrees to each other.

The range was widened by the introduction of a "starter bike," the 883cc Sportster was basic but cheap enough to lure riders of Japanese bikes over, they traded up later to the big 1340cc V-twins. There was now a vision: machinery that was modern while echoing the glorious heritage, and had modern business practices to back it up.

Let the good times roll.

THE HERITAGE NOSTALGIA IS BEST ENJOYED BY THOSE WHO DON'T MIND BEING REMINDED THAT LEATHER DEFINITELY COMES FROM A COW.

2

MAKING IT—AND MODIFYING IT

The factory may have started with a dream and a shed, as you can read in the preceding chapter, but that is not enough to keep any company afloat in the aggressive world of today. Dreams, however cleverly they are marketed, seldom survive the implacable efficiency of the Japanese. To do more than survive—to prosper—you have to stop believing all of your T-shirt slogans for a while and open your eyes.

MAKING IT
AND MODIFYING IT

One of the fascinations of the Harley-Davidson story is that it is not just a simple tale of one or more people starting a company, and that company becoming more and more successful with every year. This is much more of a human drama, with struggle, self-imposed wounds and enemy forces all playing a part in a battle that has gone one way then the other over the decades. One result of the toing and froing is that you could say the company has two faces, and for once that is not meant as

an insult. One face is in Juneau Avenue, Milwaukee, the other face, slightly wider spread, is in a Milwaukee suburb and in York, Pennsylvania.

In a residential area of Milwaukee, just behind a small shopping mall, rises a six-floor red-brick building, the headquarters of Harley-Davidson. The building has been in this shape since 1914, the year the First World War broke out, with the parts and accessories operation next door in a building erected in 1918, the year the First World War ended. All six floors used to echo to the sound of the welder and the fabricator but now these are just echoes as the pen has replaced the welding torch. Executive offices on the sixth floor used to be

AN IRON-HEAD SPORTSTER THAT HAS HAD HORRIBLE THINGS DONE TO IT. YOU PROBABLY WOULDN'T LIKE THE OWNER... BUT THEN AGAIN, YOU MIGHT.

TOP JUNEAU AVENUE, MILWAUKEE HAS BEEN THE
HARLEY-DAVIDSON HUB SINCE THE END OF THE
FIRST WORLD WAR. THE ORIGINAL SHED IS
VIRTUALLY NEXT DOOR.

Engines and transmissions are now made in the
Milwaukee suburb of Wauwatosa, from where they
are transported approximately 800 miles to the
main plant in York, Pennsylvania.

where they made the frames in the 1920s, for
example. But this is not just a historic relic, this is
a vibrant building at the heart of an empire. And it
is just one block away from where the first shed
went up in 1903.

Juneau Avenue has virtually no part to play in
the actual manufacturing process, although it
naturally oversees all operations. And since The
Buyback from AMF it has overseen changes far
more radical than the launch of the Evolution
engine would suggest. In 1981, the year
of The Buyback, the Japanese were
making big inroads into everyone's market
share, and the machines being produced
with the Harley-Davidson badge were
ominously bad in terms of quality and
reliability—for example valve seats on
1979 and '80 models of the big twins had
to be replaced within a few thousand
miles on far too many machines to keep
owners happy.

LEFT INSIDE THE FACTORY, CYLINDER HEADS
FOR THE EVOLUTION MOTORS WAIT TO
BE BOLTED ON—THERE ISN'T MUCH
STOCK JUST LYING AROUND.

TOP

THE MOST SUCCESSFUL FLAT-TRACKER OF THEM ALL, THE XR750, GOT TO WEAR THE "NUMBER 1" PLATE MORE OFTEN THAN NOT, EVEN THOUGH THE FACTORY DIDN'T ALWAYS SUPPORT RACING WITH ANY ENTHUSIASM.

The fact that these sort of problems were not a worry on Japanese machines, plus a realization that maybe the Orientals were successful for more reasons than simply the famed bowl of rice a day, led the H-D management to radically revise methods and ways of thinking that had dominated for decades.

Probably the greatest change was to stock control. That sounds boring, but it underpinned the whole way of thinking, so that instead of thousands of items sitting in piles ready to go on to the assembly line, wasting space and money, parts would now arrive and go virtually straight onto the line. The Japanese used the Kanban method, a warehousing system that saved a fortune compared to the

outdated American methods. It meant that, in a perfect world, a part would arrive from an outside source or a warehouse and be fitted immediately to the machine.

The American management looked at it all, shut its collective jaw with the aid of a hand, and tried to come up with something better. The result was the ascent of M.A.N.—Materials As Needed. This meant that parts had to arrive not just at the factory, but at the right section of the factory at the right time from all the external sources. It also meant that everybody in the workforce and several hundred outside suppliers had to understand and obey the new system.

Initial scepticism dwindled in the face of the obvious increase in efficiency (made all the more remarkable by the fact that parts came in not just from factories in the U.S.A. but from all over the world, with wheels from Australia and pistons from Germany to name but two).

ANOTHER ERIK BUELL CREATION SHOWING A
SPORTSTER WITH THE CENTRAL SHOCK ABSORBER
SLUNG UNDER THE CRANKCASES—IT LOOKED GOOD
AND HANDLED BETTER THAN THE FACTORY BIKES.

With the demise of the old parts system also went
the old idea that a model would be produced on
the line for a reasonable period of time. Blanks
and dies would now be stored by the presses
rather than in a basement somewhere else, so
that the line could produce a variety of machinery
when it was needed. This sounds like a sensible,
obvious way of going about things, but to the
American way of life it was a massive change. And
it came just in time.

A classic example of the depth of change needed
was the fiberglass plant, previously the Tomahawk
Boat Company in Wisconsin. The plant was fine for
making large boats in the 1960s but the
techniques, which involved heat curing with a
shrinkage of eight percent, was really unsuitable for
producing items like fenders and saddlebags. The

IT'S HARD TO BELIEVE BUT A TRAFFIC COP
ORIGINALLY USED TO SIT IN THAT SADDLE.
THIS IS A CUSTOMIZED FXRP EX-POLICE
BIKE, WITH ARLEN NESS FAIRING AND
REAR FENDER.

ERIK BUELL USED TO WORK FOR THE FACTORY BUT LEFT TO MAKE HIS OWN HOT-FRAMED SPECIALS. THIS RR1200 WAS PRESENTED TO CART CHAMPION DANNY SULLIVAN.

shrinkage showed up the strands in the fiberglass, but H-D got around this for a while by painting the products matt black or white so it was harder to spot. By the late 1970s the factory was turning out color-coded items that were of totally unacceptable standard, leading to many complaints from everyone who had seen what the Japanese could do with the same items. Eventually, the new quality control regime arrived in the 1980s along with new materials and techniques, and now the plant turns out top-quality accessories.

Like many western industrial countries, America had its union problems in the 1970s, although

Vaughn Beals, who became President of AMF Harley-Davidson in 1975, did try to get some dialog between management and unions. By the 1980s this dialog had become a partnership, with the workforce given more responsibility—and accepting it. Quality Circles are now in force, where workers and managers voluntarily take courses that teach them about new technologies and which impose tighter disciplines not just on the production line but on themselves as well. Self-discipline always works better than discipline imposed from the outside and, anyway, the Harley-Davidson ethic is hardly that of someone who conforms because he is told to, is it?

The workforce of about 2,500 has some good toys to play with, as well. The AMF years may have been disastrous in some ways, but at least they put some money in. The Capitol Drive building in the Milwaukee

THE FLAME-JOB PAINT
SCHEME SEEMS TO
SURVIVE EVERY
DECADE AND
REMAINS ONE OF THE
CLASSIC DESIGNS IF
YOU LIKE THAT SORT
OF THING. THIS IS A
TYPICAL DAYTONA
FLAMER.

THE STURGIS 50TH
COMMEMORATIVE BIKE,
BUILT BY ENGLISHMAN
JOHN REED, SHOT AT
CUSTOM CHROME IN
CALIFORNIA. A CUSTOM
RETRO TO TAKE YOUR
EYES OUT.

 ONE OF THE CREATIONS BY ARLEN NESS THAT SHOWS WHY HE IS SO FAMOUS. THIS DOUBLE-ENGINED SHOW-BIKE CAN DEFINITELY BE RIDDEN

suburb makes the engines and transmissions with the help of a massive monster that machines the cases for five-speed transmissions. This machine cost $4.5 million and was the most expensive single machine that AMF ever bought.

Elsewhere, in the York production process, there are machines for everything: grinding, welding,

painting, plating and finishing. There is one construction shift a day, eight hours in which about 160 motorcycles will be completed. Those are the sort of figures—20 motorcycles an hour—which would hardly show a blip on a Honda production line but Harley-Davidson is, finally, aiming not at mass production but at wealthy middle classes. Crucially, quality control is in the hands of every

 YELLOW IS THE NEW COLOR FOR HARLEY CUSTOMS, ALTHOUGH IT APPEARS COINCIDENTAL THAT THE HAMSTERS, OF WHOM ARLEN NESS IS THE MOST FAMOUS MEMBER, ALSO USE THE SAME COLOR.

A FROG HOG. THIS AMAZING BIKE WAS MADE BY TECHNO PLUS FROM FRANCE, AND WON TOP AWARD AT THE 1994 KENT, ENGLAND, CUSTOM BIKE SHOW.

A FROG HOG. THIS AMAZING BIKE WAS MADE BY TECHNO PLUS FROM FRANCE, AND WON TOP AWARD AT THE 1994 KENT, ENGLAND, CUSTOM BIKE SHOW.

worker on the line, although workers expert in statistical process control will monitor the evolving machine all the way down the line. This is still a process that uses a great deal of human input. For example, the frames may be painted by electrostatic paint booths, but they go back to be checked, and any missing paint is touched in by hand. Most tank and fender striping is also done by hand with templates and paint pencils, and decals are all applied by a steady hand and an experienced eye.

At the end of the line the bikes are run up by a test rider and a bank of machines before being crated and shipped out in the factory's own trucks. Any that fail the final inspection are returned to the Harley Hospital for remedial work. With much of the work now done in-house, with quality control markedly improved due to both operator performance and the installation of machinery to detect errors all along the line, the end result is a machine of much higher integrity and quality; a fact corroborated by the dramatic fall in the number of warranty claims.

But of course the end of the production line is not the end of the line. The factory itself produces a multitude of subtly different models and of course owns companies that will make your Harley different to the next one off the line. Even that is not enough for many, who want something so individual that they know nobody else will ever have anything like it. Such people do not ride Hondas.

Some people may have a go at customization themselves with the usual flame jobs, big carbs, high or flat bars and all the rest but, for a really top-dollar job, you have to go to the professionals.

Many of the pros go back to the 1960s, when this form of self-expression just about started, although it seemed to start absolutely flat out. This was when young men like Arlen Ness would do a day

job then go to his little office in the evening to design parts like his Ramhorn handlebars. And it was in the days when he would turn up at the office in the evening after a day's work and find people in line for his bars—that certainly got him thinking and designing on a bigger scale.

Now he is probably the most famous builder of them all, a man who looks at a stock Harley as a starting point, not the finished product. Sometimes working with his son, Cory, Arlen has created some of the most radical customs, but the Ferrari bike must rank as the most powerful statement he is ever likely to make. Harleys are hardly known for their bashful, self-effacing image, but this monster takes the biscuit and anything else it damn well pleases. John Harmon cases, with massive bores filled by Chevy V8 pistons, give 128 cubic inches and power to match. That wasn't enough. Special heads and extra-large valves went on the top. That wasn't enough. Arlen added a Magnuson blower and two big carbs—to each cylinder. Still not enough. So each cylinder got its own nitrous oxide bottle. That was more than enough.

 TOP THE NESS CONVERTIBLE CAN HAVE THE VALENCED COVERS REMOVED TO CHANGE THE LUXURY LINER TO A STREET DIGGER.

The whole machine, with solid tail and upside-down forks, was then clothed in aluminum panels with echoes of the Ferrari Testarossa in both its sculpted lines and the color. To put the whole thing in perspective, it has the power to beat a five-liter Mustang and a rear tire bigger than that found on a Ferrari Testarossa. And it gets ridden.

A passer-by was so stunned to see it at the Daytona Speed Week with dirt on its tires that he remarked that actually using it on the street was like playing volleyball in the Sistine Chapel because the ceiling is high enough. Not that Michaelangelo (the artist, not the turtle) ever rode a Harley, although everyone knows that the main man depicted on the Sistine ceiling certainly does.

A motorbike mimicking an exotic Italian car is just one sign of how far customs have come in the last 30 years or so. Back in the early days you didn't need to do much more than bolt on a pair of handlebars that soared up higher than your head, a seat that let you lay back, and a pair of straight-through pipes. A stars-and-bars paint job on the tank wouldn't hurt any either. The riding position

that this pushed you into may have looked absurd to Europeans but on long American freeways it made a lot of sense. You weren't getting anywhere fast on your old Shovelhead so why not lay back and enjoy the view and the languorous thudding of that big V-twin?

Now many of the customs have come down instead of going up. Choppers have been chopped back to give a much more muscular, denser look to the bike, with flat bars and engines, frames and bodywork often in the same sort of color. Bellypans have made an appearance to accentuate all that low-down bulk and heft, making you notice even more just how massive those 1340cc crankcases are. Current trends are partly influenced by the hot-rod background of many of the top creators, so everything is now lowered to give a street dragster look. The other main look is a sort of luxury liner, with fiberglass draped over the machines that again accentuates the sheer length and volume of the bikes.

Although people were customizing bikes all over the world in the 1960s—like the cafe racer look that was hot in Britain at that time—the West Coast, and southern California in particular, is regarded as one of the hot-beds, if not the birthplace, of customizing. San Francisco's Bay Area is still the mecca for those who need something different. It is also home to an unlikely sounding bunch—the Hamsters. This loose affiliation of top customizers, not surprisingly, has Arlen Ness as one of its leading members. Their uniform is a yellow T-shirt with the logo, although one member has gone further and painted his helicopter yellow, with the furry logo on the side—now that is a chopper! By coincidence, three of Ness's recent customs have all been painted in bright yellow, and show the breadth of options available. A Knucklehead chopper, a street dragster and a big tourer are all unmistakably customs, all unmistakably yellow, and they are all working machines.

But of course Arlen Ness does not have it all to himself. People like Ron Simms, Bob Dron, Donnie Smith, Pete Chapouris and Bob Bauder are making bikes that are modern and thrilling while also echoing and re-echoing the earlier, classic customs. And let's not forget the zany one-offs like Englishman John Reed, who can build a Harley that would take your

eyeballs out. He used to live and work in the U.K. but now works for Custom Chrome in California, having replaced rain with sunshine—it shows in his work.

Many customs, whether done by the pros or by owners, can take years to complete—assuming that they can ever be finally "finished." They are flash but not flash-in-the-pan, with people putting large chunks of both their income and their life into their labors of love, so that it becomes a statement about themselves just as much as a motorbike. In fact it almost becomes more than that, it is not even a motorbike, not even a Harley-Davidson, it is art. Art on the move. Find that hard to accept? Like the T-shirt says: "If you have to ask—you wouldn't understand."

JAMES DEAN HAS BEEN THE INSPIRATION FOR MANY BIKES AND CARS, INCLUDING THIS SHOW-WINNING SOFTTAIL CONVERSION.

3

HOGS AND ANGELS

When did it all start? Hell's Angels going on toy runs, collecting cuddly toys for sick children. Angels implicated in drug running, stolen bike rings, the full range of crimes. Angels hanging out in their clubhouses all over the world, drinking beer, talking quietly about the old days. Did it start in the 1960s, with the famous book by Hunter S. Thompson, who spent a year with the Hell's Angels in California? Did it start in 1947, when a regular motorcycle club meet turned into a media riot at Hollister? Or did it start in the years before that, the Second World War?

HOGS AND ANGELS

You just have to look at the insignia—skulls, death, flames, SS runes—to see the influence the Second World War had on a generation of young men. The drama, excitement and terror of the war was replaced by a dull inaction, unemployment and the tedium of daily life. The motorbike, as always, represented an escape, a release valve. Many

settled down, faced up to the new life, but many others found it unacceptable and turned to the outlaw life, drinking, riding fast and cutting loose whenever they could. They all rode bikes, and they all rode Harley-Davidsons.

The two sides, straight riders out to have a good time, and the more rowdy element out to have a good time their way, met at Hollister in California on July 4, 1947. It was just going to be another clubman's meeting over the long holiday weekend, but it ended up with 500 police officers moving in

BEDROLL, BEARD AND BIKE—THE GERMAN HELMET TELLS YOU WHERE HE'S COMING FROM, BUT HE HASN'T GOT ANY COLORS SO HE'S NO ANGEL.

A SUNNY RIDE IN THE NEW MEXICO MOUNTAINS LEAVES YOUR CARES BEHIND— NOTE THE READY SMILES THAT DENOTE "NO ATTITUDE."

to quell the disturbances. *Life* magazine got hold of the story and ran a picture of a drunken rider brandishing a bottle of beer on its cover and, finally, biking hit the headlines around the world. It wasn't quite how many bikers wanted to be portrayed.

Life ran the picture again in 1972 and this time the howls of anguish from the mainstream biking community filled most of the subsequent Letters pages— testimony from people like actor Keenan Wynn went on to complain that out of 4,000 people there only about 500 had caused trouble. The press ignored the 3,500—the other 500 made a better story, and soon there were more of them.

If you are going to be a bad boy you can't zip about on a commuter bike, you have to have a big beast that frightens old ladies of either gender. A Harley-Davidson V-twin was the only option. It was no coincidence that the biker brandishing

his bottle on the cover of *Life* magazine was on a Harley, but it was also symbolic in its condition. Gone were the fairing, screen, massive front fender and all the other accessories with which mainstream bikers like to adorn their machines. The look was to strip off everything unnecessary, leaving a functional, gaunt machine that suited the rider's image and needs.

◀ **LEFT** SAM SHADES WAS GETTING SICK OF CONSTANTLY WASHING AND IRONING HIS T-SHIRTS AND SPENT AGES WORKING OUT HOW TO AVOID SUCH CHORES.

By the 1960s the Hell's Angels had spread, with chapters forming around the U.S.A. But the most famous was at Oakland, California, the chapter started by Sonny Barger and immortalized by Hunter S. Thompson in his book *Hell's Angels*. He lived with them for a year and had, shall we say, an interesting time. Sonny Barger drew the threads of outlaw groups together and made the Hell's Angels a significant

 THE VIETNAM VETS MOTORCYCLE CLUB ROLL IN TO RED RIVER, NEW MEXICO FOR THEIR ANNUAL MEMORIAL DAY RIDE.

force, for good or bad. Along with sidekicks like Skip, Magoo and Terry the Tramp he became famous, to the point where they actually played themselves in the road movie *Hell's Angels 69*.

The sub-culture they spawned had many side-effects, not the least of which was that they had to

 SINGER JOHNNY PAYCHECK AND SENATOR BEN "NIGHTHORSE" CAMPBELL WITH SHARON AND SONNY BARGER IN 1994 CELEBRATING THE LIFTING OF SONNY'S PAROLE RESTRICTIONS.

fend for themselves and so set up their own organizations. The Harley-Davidson factory wanted nothing to do with outlaw groups and so tried to ignore them. Normal retail and servicing outlets wouldn't work on their bikes, which forced them to set up their own outlets and servicing with their own imaginative supply lines. They literally became a law unto themselves.

Sonny Barger eventually went to jail, and didn't come out until 1992, when he was reunited with Sharon Barger, who is referred to in their circles as the First Lady of biking. Many other original Hell's Angels are either dead or getting older now. Many have stayed Angels all their adult lives, since to them the Hell's Angel chapter represents family, security and brotherhood. They know that there is always somewhere to go, and always someone to back you up if you get into trouble. They joined at 21 years of age, the minimum requirement, after a period as a "prospect," and they will stay in the Angels until they die. As a prospect you are expected to "show class," whatever that might entail, before you are accepted into a chapter.

As a group, the Angels are getting older, although younger men are still joining, and consequently, as a group, they

LEFT

NOW WHAT KIND OF BIKE COULD A GUY LIKE THIS POSSIBLY RIDE. YOU COULD SAY A HONDA... BUT NOT TO HIS FACE.

are less active, less angry than they were. The war was a long time ago, before many of the younger members were even born, and the Hell's Angels have probably had the worst thing happen to them—they have almost become establishment figures. Even their patch of skull with wings is no longer a symbol just of rebellion—it is now a copyright symbol.

But of course, wars keep right on happening and the second big attack on the American psyche, the Vietnam War, had a broadly similar effect to the Second World War. It was a war that messed up the minds of a lot of young men, who came home to find themselves ignored, unrecognized by medals or thanks. Yet again, for the second time in 30 years, the Harley-Davidson motorbike

BELOW ▼

DAYTONA IS THE BACKDROP TO A CONSTANT CAVALCADE OF RIDERS TRAWLING UP AND DOWN MAIN STREET, LIVING OUT THEIR FANTASIES OUT OF THE OFFICE.

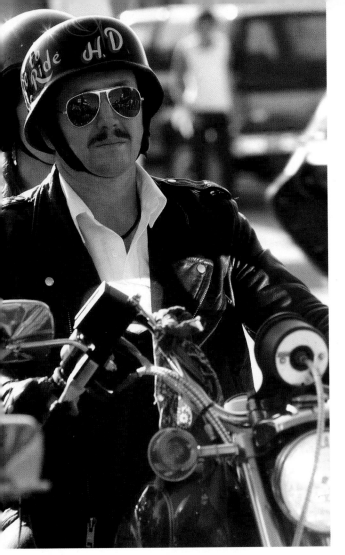

All of them ride Harley-Davidsons and, in the case of middle-aged Hell's Angels, they may have been riding numerous bikes over quite a few decades. To the Angels, this has been very much a one-way deal. The factory's history is littered with years when things went horribly wrong, or nearly went to the brink. Sales have been dreadful, models have been awful and awfully put together and the public has stayed away in droves, either because they didn't have any money, like in the Depression, or because the company was not offering the right thing at the right time. Throughout all this, the thousands of Hell's Angels have stayed faithful to the Harley fold, never riding anything else. Their devotion to the cause is hardly likely to be recognized by Harley-Davidson.

Instead the company did a very strange thing, since it spent so much time ignoring the Hell's Angels. It copied them.

In 1983 it formed the Harley Owners Group or HOG. All you had to do to join was buy a new Harley-Davidson, and a small fee made you, your spouse and the children a part of a worldwide club. The idea was to get more riders involved with motorcycling generally, so members received newsletters, emergency back-up, touring packs and all the things that made it easier to pack up the bike and get on the road. A fly-and-ride program was started so that the more adventurous traveler could leave his bike at home, fly to places as diverse as Hawaii or Germany and then rent a Harley-Davidson for a reasonable fee.

Just as important, members would get invitations to ride-outs and rallies that would only be open to them. Then there was the added advantage of getting their own reception area at the really big events like Sturgis and Daytona as well as the road racing series. All you had to do was buy a bike. The scheme took off, with more than 90,000 people

reached out a friendly hand and took them all on board. The Vietnam Vets are now a high-profile group, often seen at conventions, toy runs and anywhere else where groups of motorbikes congregate. They're definitely not Hell's Angels, but it's almost uncanny the effect war has had on separate generations of males.

Females can't join the Hell's Angels, nor indeed the other outlaw groups. The Angels must be the most imitated social group around, although you would have to be suffering from terminal stupidity—although you wouldn't suffer for long—to make up your own Hell's Angels patch or anything remotely like it. Those colors are as sacred as any regimental colors. Numerous other outlaw gangs have sprung up as copies of the original, like the Badidos, the Outlaws and the Sons Of Silence. All have their own colors, their own codes, and none of them allows women in. The best they can hope for is their own patch saying "property of... ." Feminism hasn't made that much progress here.

THE AMF YEARS—A SHOVELHEAD ELECTRA GLIDE FLH FROM THE MID 1970S, A TIME OF DRAMATIC UPHEAVAL IN THE AMERICAN BIKE WORLD.

AN FLH CLASSIC BETWEEN RAPID CITY AND STURGIS IN SOUTH DAKOTA. THIS IS WHAT THE WORD FREEWAY REALLY MEANS.

TOP

THE BLUE KNIGHTS IS A CLUB MADE UP OF EX-EMERGENCY SERVICES PERSONNEL, WHO STILL POLICE BIKER EVENTS. SUBTLE MACHINE, EH?

his new Ultra Classic. His fawning attitude to his superiors would be replaced by a deep sneer and his glasses replaced by contact lenses so that he could properly scan far horizons. He always wore clean underwear, though.

With his new patch on his back he could strut his stuff in the bars, although the chances of fellow HOG members, who came from the accounts department, coming to his aid in the event of trouble were pretty small. Nevertheless, he could live the dream so long as it didn't get too real, and could ride his bike, meet new people and live the life, whatever that was. No wonder the HOGs mimicked the Hell's Angels once again, with chapters being formed all over the world, from Australia to Britain to Germany. The good guys were fighting back, with massive support by the company, which was keen to improve the image of motorcycling and at the same time improve its sales.

joining by the end of the 1980s. Today that number has more than doubled.

Copying the Angels, the HOG was split into chapters and even had its own colors to be worn on the back of leathers and denim jackets and waistcoats. Thus was born a new type of rebel, enough to strike fear into the heart of the hardest Hell's Angel—enter the Weekend Warrior. This dread figure would do battle with the forces of darkness in the buying department during the week but, come Saturday, he would discard his suit and don his gleaming new black leathers and straddle

THE HARLEY OWNERS GROUP HAS CHAPTERS ALL OVER THE WORLD, INCLUDING A MAJOR ONE IN LONDON, ENGLAND.

RIGHT ▶

Logically, it is hard to see the HOG increasing too far since the whole point of it was to offset the excesses of the Hell's Angels, who were themselves reacting against an unfriendly society.

The translation from the U.S.A. to somewhere like conservative England, without the sun, the overt American friendliness and the budgets, can't always be a happy one although the rallies and the meetings still go on.

There are, of course, subtle differences. In America, HOG members are mostly blue-collar workers while in the British HOG outfits most members are white-collar because the bikes cost a lot more, not just to buy but to insure and run as well. Nevertheless the basic ideal that anyone can ride a Harley-Davidson survives the trip over the Atlantic. For example, of the two men who front the London chapter of the HOG in Britain—one is a merchant banker, the other a fireman.

They formed just one of the Harley Owner Groups that went to the 1995 Fourth European HOG Rally,

IT SURE AIN'T CALIFORNIA. THIS ELECTRA GLIDE CLASSIC WAS AT THE ENGLISH HOG RALLY AT LITTLECOTE IN THE COLD AND RAIN. AT LEAST THEY MUST HAVE ROOM FOR A CHANGE OF CLOTHES IN THERE SOMEWHERE.

which took place in rainy Bavaria, Germany. That great spokesman for the company, Willie G. Davidson was there along with about 8,000 members who had come from as far away as the United Arab Emirates and the former Communist Bloc. Along with the ride-in bike show, entertainment from rock groups and a Stud Yer Duds competition, there was the traditional ride-out. Even though it was wet, this was the biggest procession of Harley-Davidsons Europe had ever seen. Just imagine what a moving snake of Harley-Davidsons two and a half miles long must have looked and sounded like. Rolling thunder.

Riding together is one of the big social functions of the HOG, as it is of any bike group. HOG members like to take it a bit further than some, partly because they usually have the money. Where Hell's

 NEXT TO HIS HARLEY, MAN'S BEST FRIEND IS HIS DOG. ROGER THE DOG GETS HIS NOSE IN FRONT OF THE OLD ELECTRA GLIDE.

Angels stripped their bikes down in reaction to the dressers, HOG members pile them back up again with all the Touring Paks known to Harley-Davidson. The big 1340cc V-twins culminate in the FLHTC Ultra Classic Electra Glide, a bike almost as big as its title. This is what you need—full-frontal protection, luggage space big enough to take two full-face helmets, CB radio, cassette/radio and electronic cruise control. With 94Nm of torque at 3600rpm you have the guts to pull the several

 VIETNAM VETS AT SONNY BARGER'S FREEDOM PARTY. ALL EX-SERVICEMEN, THEY FIND THE CAMARADERIE MAKES UP FOR CIVILIAN BOREDOM.

hundred pounds of luggage the machine is capable of carrying. The seat area and frame-mounted luggage holders of top-box and panniers, can carry over 400lb weight, as much as a small car.

Touring is part of the lifestyle, it means that two people and, in an amazing number of cases dogs as well, can go and see America or just head away from the neighborhood for a while. They want the wind in their hair, and the sun on their faces but, since they tend to be older people, they don't want to go too far from a coffee stop, rest rooms and a comfortable hotel. This doesn't

IT DOESN'T MATTER WHAT AGE YOU ARE, YOU ARE ALWAYS WELCOME ON A HARLEY-DAVIDSON, HERE AN ULTRA GLIDE CLASSIC.

prevent them taking half of their home contents along with them, but they will often cover some pretty high mileages at a nice, steady speed. They are, at least, using their bikes for what they were intended.

They may be bikers but there is a tremendous gulf in every area of their lives between John and Betty Hog and Terry the Tramp. The difference is epitomized in their bikes, both big V-twin Harley-Davidsons. The Hog's has all its accessories bought from the factory, with as much protection from the elements as possible. The Tramp's has no bodywork and a bedroll stashed either across the back seat or under the headlamp.

Somewhere in the middle is the cruiser, a large sector of the market. This man doesn't want a Japanese bike, he doesn't want to die at 13,000rpm in top gear, he wants to take it easy, see and be seen. Harley research shows that he wants something like an FXR Super Glide with wide rear tire, comfortable saddle, and rubber mounts to separate him from the engine's vibration. This man is cruising because he wants to get away, but not too far. He is out in the open, out in the elements, away from all the cares of his life, like job, children, home and bad investments.

He won't go that far, but far enough to get the cares of the world off his shoulders as he concentrates on changing gear, winding through the turns and just feeling the wind gently tugging at his face and clothing. In his own small way he is rebelling too, briefly joining the outlaw band that is always out on the road. Harley-Davidsons get you that way.

DAYTONA AND STURGIS—PARTY TIME

Bike Week, Daytona, Florida. A combination of Hollywood, holiday and holy shrine. One reason to come here is to watch the racing, everything from big hogs to two-stroke "rice burners," circulating at speed on the banked bowl. This is where Barry Sheene famously crashed his Suzuki at 175mph, just as he was coming down from the banking in front of a television crew, but not many people saw it, and even fewer would have cared. The majority of the seething mass in town didn't come for the racing, they came for the scene. And they're part of it.

DAYTONA AND STURGIS

Thousands come from all over America and the world to take part in a spring-time spectacular that has all the ritual and complexity of a religious festival or an annual migration in the animal world. The little town bursts at the seams as they arrive singly or in groups, nearly all of them on Harley-Davidsons. In recent years there has been an increase in the number of big Japanese bikes posing around town and riding on the beach, but the purist can only sigh and shake his head at such a breach of etiquette. They clearly don't understand.

This is, after all, the great American Dream, although it wouldn't do to look too closely at this particular dream. If you nose around town there seem to be an awful lot of motor homes and trailers around, as if this was not the meeting of the young and the brave but of the old and the timid. You could be excused for thinking you had

BIKERS TALK ABOUT THE THRILL OF THE WIND IN YOUR HAIR AND THE BUGS IN YOUR TEETH, BUT LET'S NOT TAKE IT TOO FAR.

come across the Snow Birds, the old folk who migrate around the States, keeping ahead of the cold weather in their RVs.

A lot of the bikes didn't get ridden here, they arrived on trailers and off the back of motor homes, some of them with plates from thousands of miles away. You wouldn't want to ride your pristine and restored Knucklehead down from Seattle, but you are certainly going to give that impression, just as soon as you don your leathers and ride into town.

The town has trouble coping with the influx, with hotels, motels and campsites full for miles around—local traders aren't complaining. But let's assume that you found a room on the edge of town, and have freshened up for the evening. It's a nice warm evening so you can wear casual clothing—jeans and a T-shirt bearing the name of the insurance company that you work for back

"YEAH, REALLY, I'VE JUST RIDDEN MY HARLEY-DAVIDSON DOWN FROM NEW ENGLAND LIKE THIS. OH, I DIDN'T REALIZE YOU HAD A CAMERA."

home. Your wife hops on the back and you head into town for a pleasant dinner. Hold it. What do you think you're doing? Go back and start again.

Honestly, some people! Okay, get rid of the clothing you're wearing, and instead put on a pair of battered old jeans made of denim or leather—kick them round the room for a bit if they're looking too clean, and maybe smear some oil or something over parts of them. The T-shirt has to say something like "Harley Fucking Davidson," or "God rides a Harley," and should have been washed too many times so it's faded away—but it shouldn't have been washed recently. Dusty old boots and maybe a similarly dusty jacket (drop it in the yard if it's not covered enough) and you're ready to go. Now to sort your wife out.

From this moment on she's no longer your wife she's your "ol'lady" and has to dress the part. Lose the slacks and Ralph Lauren shirt. A bikini, denim shirt and white cowboy boots is all she needs. She may not be happy with this and may complain that nobody will believe she has ridden pillion a thousand miles dressed like that. Ignore this—no pain, no gain. A pair of helmets, two pairs of dark glasses and you're ready. No; one last little detail—slap a stick-on tattoo onto your wife's, sorry, ol'lady's chest just above her bikini top. Now you are ready. And the kicks and slaps she's giving you only add to that authentic look.

LIFE'S A BEACH, DAYTONA STYLE. CUSTOMS AND STRIPPED-DOWN HARLEYS ARE WHAT YOU NEED TO CRUISE DOWN FROM ATLANTIC AVENUE TO THE BEACH.

Fire up the Harley, kick up the stand, into gear and pull out into the river of rumbling metal heading into town. First off we'll go down Main Street. It may not be long but it is packed with bikes and bikers, parked or riding. Down one side, up the other, riding slowly partly because the press of traffic stops you doing anything else, partly because the cops won't let you go fast and partly because the slower you go the more people can see you. You are one of the crowd now, swamped by the rumbling of Harley-Davidsons, the yowl of a big Jap bike, the smell of thousands of exhausts, dozens of bars and restaurants. Where to now?

McDonald's or Denny's Diner isn't really good enough, but there is quite a choice as the event gets bigger every year, now spreading north up to Ormond Beach and south to New Smyrna Beach. Time for a beer, so head for the Iron Horse Saloon and maybe the Boot Hill Saloon. They look intimidating and there are signs pointing out some

LEFT SPORTSTER FIRED UP, BIKINI AND BOOTS ON, TATTOOS IN PLACE, WE'RE READY FOR A CRUISE DOWN MAIN STREET, DAYTONA.

of the things they don't want—colors, weapons and attitude among them—but you can get a cold beer, no sweat. You'll be rubbing shoulders with big dudes, mean and vicious looking, with their shades on even inside the bar. Tattoos bulge as big biceps move the ever-present beer bottle up to a head that seems to be 90 percent hair. The men are even worse.

In reality many of the people are not Hell's Angels nor outlaw bikers, but hospital porters from Des Moines and accountants from Disneyland, out to live a fantasy for a week a year. Mind you, the one you pick on might be the real thing, so it's not surprising that the town sees little violence or real trouble throughout Bike Week. How lucky do you feel?

The cops keep a tight lid on the place all week, with a high-profile presence that is aimed to intimidate as much as anything. Main Street is so jammed with traffic that you'll be lucky to find a space to park your bike, yet someone winding up their hog even for a hundred yards is liable to find himself looking into the mirror shades of a highway patrolman within a couple of minutes.

Nowhere is this more obvious than down on the beach. It sounds like an ideal combination—sun,

sea, sand and Harley-Davidsons—but you could run faster than you could ride on the lovely yellow sands. At least your ol'lady will stop complaining about having to wear a bikini, but a Hardtail getting the gas and kicking up a rooster of sand will have a police 4WD Jeep on its tail before he can shut down. Police helicopters clatter over in low passes, to the accompaniment of gestures and catcalls from the bikers, but the iron hand never softens.

Mind you, many worthy citizens really seem to believe that if it wasn't for the aggressive stance taken by the police the whole town would degenerate into a hell-hole where people actually enjoyed themselves. Those who don't get the attention of the cops obviously see them differently to those on the bikes, none more so than the local Chamber of Commerce, who wanted to reward the Chief of Police for his force's leniency and restraint. They obviously thought hard for a suitable present and gave him a gold-plated Winchester rifle.

BELOW ▼ ELECTRA GLIDES GIVE YOU SO MUCH FIBERGLASS TO COVER THAT EVEN THE MOST MANIC OWNER CAN NEVER REALLY RUN OUT OF A SURFACE TO DEFACE.

As light falls the smell of Harley oil mixes with the dust in the air and aroma from BBQs, a powerful cocktail that makes you want to move on. The Boot Hill Saloon, Dirty Harry's, Froggy's Saloon and, of course, the Rat's Hole where you can see more custom bikes than your eyeballs can cope with. Big Daddy Rat started the custom shows during Bike Week, although there is now competiton at the Boardwalk Custom Show down by the ocean. By now you may have had enough alcohol and want to just wander up and down watching the people and all the exciting ways in which their money is taken off them.

Decorating is a major theme, both for the body and for the bike. Tattoo artists are busy under the lights, bringing dragons, ladies and bikes to colorful but painful life on any part of the body that is proferred and that is big enough. Skulls, mythical heroes and scantily dressed heroines all jostle on backs and arms and legs with messages of eternal faith to the Harley-Davidson cause. People wouldn't put up with the pain of having Kawasaki tattooed across their chest, but for the Yankee big twin they'll lie still while the needles probe and dye.

GET 'EM YOUNG. AT STURGIS, SOUTH DAKOTA, YOU DON'T NEED TO WEAR HELMETS, WHEREAS DOWN AT DAYTONA, FLORIDA THEY ARE COMPULSORY.

But everyone is determined to ignore all this and just have a good time. You can sunbathe on the beach during the day, so long as you keep an eye out for the bikes, stroll along Atlantic Avenue looking at the waves and the babes and then hop on the hog and head off for some entertainment. Of course you need a beer, so you can call in at the Iron Horse Saloon for a cold one, but you can also buy T-shirts with suitable slogans, listen to the bands or just chill out. And, if you can stand it, you can watch the saloon's famous Wall of Death in action, but, remember kids, don't try this at home.

HARLEY-DAVIDSON RIDERS DON'T GET THE DAYTONA BEACH TO THEMSELVES, BUT IT IS STILL THE SPIRITUAL MOUNT FOR THOSE IN THE KNOW.

TOP THIS WAS ONCE AN ELECTRA GLIDE. FITTINGLY, THIS RAT BIKE IS PHOTOGRAPHED AT THE RATS HOLE IN STURGIS, WHERE THERE IS A WHOLE SHOW CATEGORY FOR RAT BIKES.

And wouldn't it be selfish just to think of yourself? After a fresh tattoo for you, you gotta think of your hog. Painters and pin-stripers are on call on the sidewalks to add some new lines and color to your beast's gas tank, or they'll do the whole bike if you have the time and the money.

It's all such a kaleidoscope of people and events, with a Christian bikers get-together next door to a gay biker's bar, an elderly couple who have obviously toured in on their Electra Glide sitting at the lights next a girl who is wearing a helmet and bikini, and a plastic surgeon from LA drinking in a bar next to a Hell's Angel from New York. The uniting force is the bike, and that is inevitably a Harley-Davidson.

Everyone seems to party day and night, with music and sideshows everywhere. The sidewalks are alive with hustlers selling gipsy jewellery, clothing and leather goods, while others wander around being as weird as they can, with a python around the neck, a stovepipe on the head and a girlfriend

BELOW THIS LADY USED TO TURN UP TO STURGIS EVERY YEAR WITH HER HUSBAND. NOW, MANY YEARS LATER, SHE STILL COMES TO MAINTAIN THE TRADITION.

who rips off her bikini top every time a camera is aimed in her direction.

Of course, if you find this offensive you can always retire a little way to the Cabbage Patch camp site, where you can watch the tasteful event known as the Women's Coleslaw Wrestling Competition. This competes with the women's Wiener eating competition for good taste, but there you go. There is something for everyone.

The festival is not seen as a problem by local storekeepers, and bar owners, who make a lot of

continent. Sturgis in South Dakota is home of the largest motorcycle rally in the world. It may not have the headline-grasping image of Daytona but it sure is big. 1990 was the year of the 50th Sturgis rally, and around 350,000 people turned up for the celebration. Harley-Davidson doesn't make a bike called a Daytona, but it has made a model called Sturgis.

The event shares some similarities with Daytona; they both feature hundreds of thousands of bikers, many of them on Harley-Davidsons, there is a Main Street in both which is the focal point for the bikers,

money, see a lot of bikes and get virtually no trouble in return. What the good folk of the town dread is the following week, when it's the Spring Break. Then thousands of fresh-faced college kids come to town. Less mature and with less money than the bikers, it is the kids who trash the place, wrecking hotels, getting into brawls and generally acting like spoiled adolescents. By then the camera crews, photographers and journalists out for a sensational story have, of course, gone home.

If you want an event that concentrates on fun rather than flesh then you should ride out of Daytona, Florida to the other side of the

LIGHTS, ACTION, SOUND—MAIN STREET DAYTONA AT NIGHT. YOU HAVE TO ADD THE CONSTANT SOUNDTRACK OF ROLLING THUNDER, DAY AND NIGHT.

both have racing taking place during the week and both are venues for a seriously good time. The Black Hill Motorcycle Classic in Sturgis is a bit more of a cultural event, with ride-outs replacing hanging out at the bars. Sure, the Main Street is like that at Daytona, bikers cruising up and down day and night, with the usual array of stands and vendors taking up every single spare space between stores, sidewalks and intersections. They'll sell you everything from

MAIN STREET, STURGIS: "WELL, OFFICER, IT'S A HARLEY-DAVIDSON AND I JUST KNOW I LEFT IT AROUND HERE SOMEWHERE. CAN YOU SEE IT?"

TYPICAL DAYTONA ACTION—THE BOOT HILL SALOON, OPPOSITE THE FAMOUS CEMETERY. MOST OF THE ACTION CENTERS AROUND THE BARS AND

MAIN & INSET

THE WEIRD TURBULENCE BEHIND THE SCREEN ISN'T HELPING THESE MENS' BEARDS. YOU REALLY DO GET LOTS OF BUGS IN THE BEARDS AFTER A RIDE.

HOG HEAVEN, DAYTONA, A CAR PARK THAT IS ONLY OPEN TO HARLEY-DAVIDSONS OF ANY SIZE, AGE OR COLOR.

leather jeans to an oil change, but one good point in the town's favor is its excellent variety of places to eat. The area is rich in history and this is reflected in the food you can tuck away, everything from Indian tacos to buffalo burgers.

The rally takes place in August, when it can get really hot and you don't have the ocean to cool off in. Instead you can loaf around town or get out on your Harley and see the sights. The area is packed with history and geography and, during the week, pretty much any road you head out on will have other bikes going or coming. Group rides are popular but this is a good week to just head out on your own because you're bound to meet other people, who want to talk about the places or the Harleys you are both sure to be on.

Within a day's ride you can see the Devil's

Tower, that weird column of solidified magma which was seen in Spielberg's *Close Encounters Of The Third Kind*. Not far away you can meet four presidents at Mount Rushmore, although their expressions are a bit stony, then you could see the Ellesworth Air Force Base with its B-52 bombers, the Badlands, the Custer Monument and Deadwood, where Wild Bill Hickock was gunned down.

The scenery between all these historic places is fabulous and the constant flow of bikes makes it all the more interesting, but maybe we should head back to town for a bit. We're going to look at women again, but this time they're not covered in coleslaw. The female of the species has been buying more and more bikes as time has gone by, and now women have their own magazine, *Harley Women*—you just know there isn't going to be a *Yamaha Women* magazine. *Harley Women* organized a Ladies Day at Sturgis in 1989, at which more than 300 women on Harley-Davidsons turned up, some of them with men or dogs in tow.

There isn't a lot of space in town so Harley-Davidson has a headquarters at the Rushmore Plaza, where you can see women again, this time

MAIN STREET, STURGIS IS CLOSED TO TRAFFIC OTHER THAN THE TWO-WHEELED KIND BUT, EVEN SO, PARKING UP IS STILL A PROBLEM.

the Ladies Of Harley. These are serious owners and riders and they have their own program for the week, including bike servicing seminars, and even a Stud Your Duds Workshop. Clothing gets a good airing since the whole range of Harley-Davidson gear is on show along with the complete model line-up of bikes. The Harley Owners Group get a good deal on parts and even food, helping make it worthwhile to own a Harley-Davidson. Big bands like ZZ Top, put on by the factory, certainly help the week along—not that it needs much help.

In Daytona you get the beach, the bars and the babes, while Sturgis has the bikes, the culture and the scenery. Which one you fancy says a lot about what you are, but you don't have to decide which one to go to. Daytona's at Easter, Sturgis in August—go to both and party on.

TYPICAL STURGIS ACTION—RIDING OUT ON THE WIDE OPEN ROADS. IN THE BACKGROUND IS BEAR BUTTE, A SACRED SPOT FOR THE SIOUX.

5

SPEED

Harley-Davidsons were as fast as anything else out there for decades, until the Japanese came along with their ring-a-ding two-strokes and high-revving four-strokes. Although there have been some spirited attempts to fight back by individuals and companies, the races where Harleys are most likely to win now are in series where only Harley-Davidsons can enter. Drag racing and one-marque track racing are just two areas where Harleys are once again thrilling the crowds, but the big V-twin may soon be back in the limelight of the World Superbike series.

If you look at World Superbikes now, with their shrieking four-cylinder, multi-valve, all-alloy construction, with chassis and brakes at almost Grand Prix levels of sophistication, it seems incredible to think that a Harley-Davidson V-twin could compete with them, yet that is what is going to happen. As the Year 2000 approaches, it is worth remembering that the V-twins have been racing for nearly all of the century. Few can match that record.

It is nearly 90 years since Bill Harley penned the design of the first 45-degree V-twin, but the first racing bikes would have put the fear of God into a modern racer used to disk brakes all round, variable rising-rate suspension and massive radial tires. The first official 61cu in (1000cc) V-twin racers were built for the infamous Wrecking Crew, a disparate group who enthralled the crowds in the period around the First World War. The

 FLYING THE FLAG. BEFORE THE SERIOUS RACING STARTS THIS STUNT RIDER STRUTS HIS STUFF FOR THE CROWD.

 TOP

A TYPICAL SWAP MEET AT DAYTONA, WITH A BOARD RACER FROM 1920. THIS IS LIVING HISTORY, WHERE YOU CAN LOOK, TOUCH AND BUY CLASSIC BIKES.

machines were quick, with a top speed over 100mph thanks to eight valves and compression so high that it sometimes took three men to bump-start them. Direct drive, no suspension and a magneto cut-out switch on the bars as the only form of braking meant these were only suitable for riders like the Wrecking Crew. They formed the backbone of a Harley attack that took every road racing victory in 1921. This was in a period of swashbuckling adventure, where courage made up for deficiencies in machine

 LEFT

PART OF THE DAYTONA SPEED BOWL, WITH THE MOTORCROSS TRACK IN THE MIDDLE. THE BIG BANKED SECTIONS ARE FURTHER ROUND THE COURSE.

and track. Crew members like Ralph Hepburn, Otto Walker and Ray Weishaar risked their lives routinely on rough, dusty courses around the United States. Weishaar brought a mascot into the team—a small piglet that had its own uniform and appears from the old photos to like being fed Coca Cola. Is this the earliest hog?

By the time of the Two-Cam at the end of the Roaring Twenties the Wrecking Crew was wrecked, but rudimentary front suspension and braking were introduced, which helped control the 74cu in power, capable of taking riders like

race his Harley at an average of over 100mph, he became the champion for years not on a big V-twin but on his little 350cc Peashooter. In 1935 he rubbed in his superiority by winning all 13 rounds of the American Motorcycle Association (AMA) National Championship.

The following year he went for the speed record at Daytona Beach. There is a posed studio shot of him complete with white shirt and tie, on the 61cu in overhead-valve Special with a lot of bodywork that was meant to help with aerodynamics. In the event he made the run

the great Joe Petrali to around 120mph. As early as 1925 Petrali was averaging over 100mph for an entire race.

Joe was one of the most famous riders in the 1920–'30s, getting through the Depression as a works rider on a salary of $40 a week. He was National Hill Climb Champion in the 1930s for six straight years and could always be relied on to test specials or to go for speed records. And on the board track races he was king. The first man to

HARLEY-DAVIDSON RIDERS LINE UP FOR THE START OF THE HALF-MILER AT OKLAHOMA, USING THE ROTAX SINGLE-CYLINDER ENGINES NORMALLY USED FOR QUARTER-MILERS.

without the tie and without the bodywork since it upset the balance of the bike, but he still set a new record of 136mph. It was pretty much his high point, and he resigned from Harley-Davidson in 1938 after arguing about money and the company's lack of racing program.

Harley-Davidson. Wrestling a 45cu in V-twin round a cinder or wooden track may have been one thing, but to fight one over a dirt course, leaping it over obstacles, would definitely have been another.

Hillclimber Windy Lindstrom won more than 300 events over a quarter of a century period from 1925 onward, and he didn't do that by taking it easy. While others used specially lengthened frames to help keep the front wheel looping over behind the back wheel, Windy just rode a stock 45cu in or 74cu in Harley-Davidson. He wound the throttle up and kept it there as the machine bucked and leapt up the rough hillside, and if it looked like he was about to loop it he wouldn't back off the throttle, he'd just hit the ignition kill button for a second before the power poured back in.

THE BIG XRS, WHICH ARE TOO MUCH FOR THE SMALLER CIRCUITS, SHOWN HERE LETTING LOOSE AT A NIGHT RACE—HONDA PAID HARLEY-DAVIDSON THE GREATEST COMPLIMENT BY COPYING THEIR ENGINE AND COMING UP WITH A V-TWIN 750CC RACER.

Many would retire with their memories but when the famous Spruce Goose briefly flew in 1947 as testimony to whatever it was that made Howard Hughes decide to build the biggest aircraft in the world, Petrali was on board. He was head of the millionare's flight services by then, and moved on to become a respected official for the United States Auto Club.

It must have been quite an occasion for a man who set a speed record just in three figures 45 years before to stand on the endless salt flats at Bonneville in 1970 as official timer and see a Harley-Davidson Streamliner, piloted by Cal Rayborn, blast past at 265mph.

His career was based upon Harleys and Indians, but the bikes remind us that in those days there weren't that many specialist machines around. Whether you were competing in just about any type of racing, from flat track to drag racing to road racing to hill climbing, you often ended up using the same base machine, and that machine was often a big and heavy

INDOOR TT RACES ARE LIKE THE FLAT-TRACK EVENTS BUT THERE ARE A FEW JUMPS THROWN IN FOR GOOD MEASURE. THESE HOGS FLY WELL.

Wild men like Lindstrom, Petrali, the Wrecking Crew and many others helped keep the Harley-Davidson name alive anywhere that competitive bikers got together, even though the factory itself blew hot and cold in its racing commitment. All through two world wars, the Depression, the Cold War and after, crowds could be guaranteed a thrill watching courageous riders fighting to keep a big, bellowing V-twin ahead of the opposition. It's what legends are made of.

But the coming of the modern, sanitized era certainly didn't stop the Wild West attitude. Flat track racing has long been a H-D domain, a form of racing where the mile or half-mile track is simply a matter of two straights and two 180-degree bends. TT courses are a variation on this, with a couple of jumps and tight turns thrown in, but the basic format requires the riders to be expert at rear-wheel steering since the powerful bikes get up to high speed on the straights but have no brakes to slow them for the turns. Instead the rider has to pitch it in, slewing speed off sideways as the bike struggles for adhesion and the rider's inside foot helps keep the machine balanced ready to acclerate out of the corner. Misjudge your approach and there is no front brake lever to help you knock off your speed—you're not going to be coming out of this particular turn.

In the 1940s, '50s and '60s, a succession of Harley-Davidsons held sway—the 45cu in WR then the KR with TT versions of each. The low-compression, side-valve WR kept the foreign opposition at bay. But that opposition was minimal anyway due to a restriction on compression ratio for other bikes, like Triumphs, which needed decent compression to work properly. By the time of the KR in the 1950s the situation was getting ridiculous, with the AMA, heavily influenced by Harley-Davidson, doing everything in its power to massage the rules so that Harleys kept on winning.

CLASSIC VINTAGE RACING STARTS OFF RACE WEEK AT DAYTONA EVERY YEAR, PROVIDING NOSTALGIA AGAINST THE THROTTLE STOP.

The 750cc (45cu in) KR was able to compete whereas Triumphs, Nortons and Ariels, among others, were kept down to 500cc by a dismal ruling about the differences between side-valve and overhead-valve engines.

It wasn't even as if the KR was a good bike—it didn't handle as well as the opposition and its barrels distorted after only 200 miles, requiring a rebore which, purely coincidentally, took it out from 744 to 767cc, a useful increase in volume. It was heavy, at 385lb for the TT version, which meant that the nimbler, lighter British bikes could get away in the corners since getting round the turns on the Harleys took strength and commitment, yet it was only in 1969, when the game was well and truly up, that the biased rulings were dropped and the Harleys had to compete on equal terms. The KR won 12 out of 17 championships but that would undoubtedly have been the end of it had it not been for the new bike of 1970, the XR.

This was a machine that needed no help, no rule-bending to win and win again. Originally made with iron barrels before going over to aluminum cylinders and heads, this OHV V-twin puts out 90bhp. When you combine that with its tiny size, nimble handling and weight of under 300lb, you have an extremely practical yet potent machine.

before nearly all his many races. Often fighting teammate Scott Parker for the lead, "Springer" thrilled the fans and dominated the championship for more than a decade, always on an XR750, even when the Japanese were starting to dominate podium places in the 1980s.

The XR750 was the basis for the XR1000, which was made as a pavement bike to take on the Japanese hordes in the AMA Battle of the Twins series. Based on the XL streetbike, it produced the same power as the XR750 but had a completely different power delivery to suit it to the high-speed banking of the Daytona bowl. It was all but slung together under the watchful eye of racing director Dick O'Brien but it won the prestigious Daytona round just a few months later, in spring 1983. Jay Springsteen was the rider, showing that he could handle any type of Harley. Certainly on the dirt-tracks he didn't normally travel at 167mph as he did at Daytona.

Another dirt-tracker, Gene Church, took over the reins of the bike known as "Lucifer's Hammer."

▲ **TOP** THE 883CC SPORTSTER RACING CLASS HAS PROVEN A REAL WINNER, WITH ALMOST UNBELIEVABLY FAST, CLOSE RACING TO THRILL THE FANS.

You only get a back brake and yet you have full throttle with just quarter of a turn of the wrist. It has won everything, everywhere, and in its latest form, is still fending off 750cc V-twin Hondas on the big dirt circuits.

On this machine a succession of works and private riders reached the top of their professions, in quarter-mile, half-mile and mile dirt-track and TT. The 1970s and '80s saw a string of riders like Cal Rayborn, Mert Lawwill, Randy Goss and of course Jay Springsteen.

Springsteen and the XR went together in a partnership that obliterated everyone else for years. He was a natural talent let loose, although he suffered terrible stomach pains

LUCIFER'S HAMMER BEAT ALL OPPOSITION IN THE BATTLE OF THE TWINS SERIES FOR SEVERAL YEARS AND WAS SPONSORED BY THE HARLEY OWNERS GROUP—IT IS SHOWN HERE IN THEIR COLORS. **RIGHT ▶**

The bike had been around in one form or another for about ten years, but the Harley Owners Group sponsored it and paid to get it really sorted out. It looked big and bulbous compared to some of the Oriental opposition but it was in fact a balanced package, painted in the HOG colors of brown, gold and white. It worked so well that Gene Church won the Battle of the Twins championships in 1984, '85 and '86, bellowing ahead of all opposition, whatever country it came from.

The Battle of the Twins series was not designed exclusively with Harley-Davidsons in mind, but there is no doubt that it came along at a good time. In the main track events the big four-strokes were being wiped out by the two-strokes in the works Suzukis and Yamahas, later to be joined by demon Kawasakis and Hondas.

NOT ALL HARLEY DRAGSTERS COMPETE IN THE ALL-HARLEY DRAG RACING ASSOCIATION, AND NOT ALL COMPETE IN THE STATES—THIS IRON-HEAD SPORTSTER IS AT SANTA POD, ENGLAND.

By this stage, the 1980s, two-stroke Harley-Davidsons were not a mainstream option, although back in the AMF days Walter Villa and Renzo Pasolini were works Harley-Davidson riders on two-strokes. The pair rode what was actually an Aermacchi two-stroke, water-cooled two-cylinder, and the machine was so quick that Walter Villa won the road-racing championship from 1974 to '76 on the 250cc version, taking the 350cc title in '76 for good measure. These are more Harley-Davidson wins, technically, although you won't find many who feel quite right seeing them against Harley-Davidson's name. Such confusion didn't do anyone much good—not that Walter Villa was

SIXTY THREE

THE VR1000 MAY YET BEAT THE BEST IN THE WORLD SUPERBIKE SERIES, BUT IT HAS SO MANY NEW SYSTEMS IT HAS A LOT TO SHAKE DOWN.

complaining—and the factory is keen not to see its image diluted again even at the expense of losing business partnerships. It has got the public thinking of Harley-Davidsons as big V-twins and they're not going to jeopardize that again, so what can you do if you can't play with the Japanese? Play with yourself has to be the unhappy answer.

Dragsters like Marion Owens used to do good things on his Harleys, but now the chances of a Harley-Davidson winning at drag racing have been

MIGUEL DUHAMEL AND THE VR1000 FLAT OUT, HIGH ON THE DAYTONA BANKING IN A SURPRISE APPEARANCE. THEY SHOULD SOON CAST AN EVEN LONGER SHADOW OVER THE SUPERBIKE SERIES.

radically enhanced by the formation of the All-Harley Drag Racing Association.

Similarly, for pavement racing, the formation in America and Europe of a championship dedicated to the 883cc Sportster has reaped rich dividends in terms of fan enjoyment and media exposure for what is a fairly basic, slow and pedestrian machine. The regulations for the 883 championship either in Europe or America, where it is known as Twin Sports, are very specific, allowing few changes from standard. The results are fairly astonishing, with extremely close racing that

certainly looks fast, setting lap times a lot nearer pure racing bike speeds than you'd imagine. It has thrown up the odd top rider, like Scott Zampach, who is three-times AMA Twin Sport Champion, and certainly spices up the program of any race meet, even at Daytona.

It was Daytona that first saw the new Superbike contender, in the spring of 1994. The VR1000 is being readied slowly and has spent a season competing and getting problems ironed out, both on the machine and the brand new team. One of the main problems is supplying the necessary 200 customer machines called for by the homolgation rules. Harley-Davidson needed to build seven to take part at Daytona, and the factory managed this, but 200 is taking a while, as is running a program of improvements on the VR. There is nothing wrong with

 BELOW ▼

ERIC BUELL USED TO WORK FOR HARLEY-DAVIDSON, THEN HE LEFT TO MAKE FAST, GOOD-HANDLING HARLEYS LIKE THIS 1200 SPORTSTER. NOW HARLEY'S BOUGHT HIS COMPANY!

the basic bike, which is light and handles well, but the hunt is on for a bit more horsepower to make it truly competitive with the established machines from Japan and Italy.

With 145bhp already available it shows just how competitive the championship is, but the V-twin also needs to lose a bit of weight. Given that it is only really at the beginning of its development program, with many parts still in steel or aluminum instead of titanium and carbon-fiber, this is not a big problem. Even so, this is the most radical Harley-Davidson yet, notwithstanding that it is a four-stroke V-twin. This one is liquid-cooled with four valves per cylinder actuated by double overhead camshafts. It also has fuel injection, and here there have been some problems, sufficient to stall the effort at Daytona, but not before rider Miguel Duhamel

TOP

SCOTT ZAMPACH'S 883 SPORTSTER HAS WORN THE COVETED NUMBER ONE PLATE IN THE AMA TWIN SPORT CHAMPIONSHIPS THREE TIMES—SO FAR.

BELOW ▼

CLASSIC ACTION WITHIN THE DAYTONA BOWL. THE START OF THE DAYTONA 200, WITH KENNY ROBERTS IN THE LEAD. NOTE HOW EMPTY THE STADIUM IS—EVERYONE IS OUT PARTYING.

TRICK HARLEY WITH CUSTOM FRAME, AND THE SORT OF FORKS AND BRAKES THAT WOULD BENEFIT MOST ROAD RIDERS TRYING TO SLOW 700LB WITH ONE OR TWO IRON DISCS.

managed to wring some good times out of the bike, much to the delight of the crowds who didn't even expect it to be at the race.

This could be a serious contender, with some major input from the factory. Characters involved in this all-new effort include Dick O'Brien, the former race team director, Eric Buell, a former employee who has made his own-framed racing Harleys, and Don Tilley who made "Lucifer's Hammer II," the Battle of the Twins bike from the 1980s that did 175mph.

This is quite a roll call, but it continues with some of America's greatest names as there is a real effort to keep the whole thing American. Suspension is by Penske and brakes by Wilwood, for example, two companies famously involved with IndyCar racing.

From an engineering point of view, this is the most modern Harley-Davidson ever seen, a machine packed with the latest electronics and mechanical know-how, and that is not often something you can say about Harleys. If this succeeds, and the effort put in already means we hope it does, then it could be the basis for a whole new generation of Harley-Davidsons. "Racing improves the breed" is not a maxim that is ever out of date.

STARS AND BARS

It couldn't have happened to any other company. Think of BMW cars for example. New ones are driven by executives, yuppies and those who aspire to a cold and affluent lifestyle. Old BMWs, like the last model Series 3, are driven by pimps, with gold wheels and big aerofoils that won't have much effect at side-street speed. Harley-Davidsons get driven by everyone from pimps to presidents, and you can ride an old or a new model, and it still has class. Somehow, it cuts across all barriers of race, politics, money and creed. A factory worker and his company's president won't have anything in common, yet they can both be united by the bikes they ride.

STARS
AND BARS

Harleys have had their fanatical fans ever since they first started being ridden, but it was really the Hell's Angels and the outlaw bands that first brought Harleys to the attention of the general public. The factory didn't like it, but for better or worse Hell's Angels and Harley-Davidsons were forever linked in the imagination of the nation. They rode stripped-down bikes, while the rednecks rode them with all the fairings and panniers on. Neither side was going to give up riding their favored bikes just because of the other group.

THE RED HOT CHILLI PEPPERS AND THEIR COLLECTION OF HARLEYS INCLUDES THE LEAD SINGER ANTHONY KIEDIS'S FXR EVOLUTION BIG TWIN IN THE FOREGROUND.

The media moguls soon realized the draw of the name, and of course slapped Harley-Davidsons and outlaws together. The first big effort was *The*

Wild One, the 1953 black-and-white movie that was meant to reproduce the events at Hollister from 1947. Marlon Brando was the tough, moody gang hero playing against Lee Marvin. Harley-Davidsons don't actually figure all that large in the film but they are still seen as the heroes. Even more unfathomable, then, that in the film Marlon Brando rides a Triumph Speed Twin with an upside-down M on the tank from a Matchless. Maybe that was why the movie was banned from Britain for 14 years.

By the 1960s the theme was warming up, with movies like *Wild Angels* in 1966. It is hardly an intellectual milestone, telling as it does the rambling tale of two bikers, death and orgies, but it went on to be America's official entry to the Venice film festival. It won.

That movie starred Peter Fonda as the biker, Blues, but he is best known as Wyatt in the 1969 movie *Easy Rider*. Starring Jack Nicholson with director, writer and star Dennis Hopper, this must be one of the biggest cults of all time. A line of extremely

A PANHEAD CHOPPER IDENTICAL TO THE ONE RIDDEN BY PETER FONDA IN *EASY RIDER*. HARDTAIL FRAME, FISHTAIL PIPES AND A MONSTER SET OF FORKS.

 PETER FONDA AND DENNIS HOPPER HIT THE ROAD ON THEIR PANHEADS IN *EASY RIDER*, THE CULT FILM FROM 1969 THAT DID NOTHING FOR THE IMAGE OF REDNECKS IN THEIR PICK-UPS.

fashionable women's clothing came out in 1995, featuring a leather jacket exactly like that worn by Peter Fonda in the movie—black leather with stripes of white and red on the arm and chest. About 25 years after the film, chic women are wearing clothing worn by a dirty biker in a cult movie that majored on Harley-Davidsons, sex, drugs and rock'n'roll. Amazing when you think about it.

Both Wyatt and Billy (Dennis Hopper) ride Panhead Harleys done up in the custom of the time with stars-and-bars fuel tank to match Peter Fonda's helmet, stretched forks and lots of chrome. Both men end up being blown away by the classic redneck in a pickup, but that redneck could well have had an Electra Glide back in his garage.

EVEL KNIEVEL ON ONE OF HIS TOURS OF THE UK NARROWLY AVOIDS CATCHING A BUS. WHAT HAPPENS IN THE NEXT FEW SECONDS IS ANYONE'S GUESS.

The Electra Glide became a cult vehicle within the Harley-Davidson range. Big and bouncy, it first appeared in 1965 and was the largest thing on two wheels. By the 1970s the cult had become an obsession for some, especially Robert Blake, star of the 1973 movie *Electra Glide In Blue*. The film is a touching love story between an Arizona State patrolman and his bike, although, strangely enough, he too ends the film by being blown out of the saddle, the big bike continuing on without him.

American traffic cops had been riding Harley-Davidsons since the 1930s, although by the time *Electra Glide In Blue* was made many forces were switching over to 900cc Kawasakis. However, the situation has now turned around again and the California Highway Patrol (of CHiPS fame) are now back on modified Pursuit Glides and Electra Glides, once again riding proud and comfortable on American iron.

BRANDO WITH A TRIUMPH SPEED TWIN! FROM *THE WILD ONE* BASED ON THE HOLLISTER "RIOT" OF 1947. MARLON GOT THE GIRL BUT LEE MARVIN GOT THE HARLEY-DAVIDSON.

when they went wrong. He crashed on film trying to leap the fountain at Caesar's Palace in Las Vegas, the accident scraping off skin and snapping bones so they poked into his leathers as he smashed to a halt. By 1970, fully recovered, he joined forces with Harley-Davidson and had his whole fleet of bikes and vehicles painted in the stars-and-stripes, just like Peter Fonda's bike in *Easy Rider*. Riding mostly XR750s, he made himself and the company even more famous, although it all went into a downward spiral after his jet-powered, AMF Harley-Davidson-logo'd missile crashed into the Snake River Canyon in 1974.

That was all something of a diversion, but now all the outlaw bikers who helped shape the public's consciousness about Harley-Davidsons have to share their biking with just about every celebrity in the world. Singers, actors and actresses and people who are famous simply for being famous all seem to ride or at least own a Harley-Davidson. It would be easy to say that they are all just jumping on the band-wagon, trying to buy some instant image by riding the same machinery as serious bad-ass Hell's Angels. In many cases this is doubtless true, but media folk have been riding the bikes since before the Hell's Angels were formed.

It mentions in Chapter Three that actor Keenan Wynn was incensed enough to write to the press after *Life* magazine's coverage of the Hollister "riot" of 1947. Wynn has been a life-time fan of Harley-Davidsons, first appearing on one as a bike cop in the movie *Code Two* that came out about the same time as *The Wild One*.

During the Second World War, when many people saw Harley-Davidson WLAs on newsreel footage in

Harley-Davidson management weren't all that thrilled with some of the films that came out about their products—it can't have helped that half the heroes riding Harleys seemed to get shot out of the saddle. One antidote was to concentrate on the racing side of things, not that clean fighting and an observation of the rules were much in evidence even here. Dirt-tracker Mert Lawwill, Harley's top factory rider, had cameras following him, even strapped to his helmet, throughout the 1970 AMA season as he raced at circuits all over the U.S.A. *On Any Sunday* was a good film, much enjoyed by bikers, but it had hardly any impact on the public compared to the slew of movies that showed Harley-Davidson riders as drugged, degenerate and, ultimately, dead.

One man who seemed to spend his life attempting to die on his Harley-Davidson was the most famous stunt-man of them all, Evel Knievel. He was famous for some outrageous stunts, but equally famous for

MICHAEL HUTCHENCE, LEAD SINGER WITH INXS, LOUNGES ON HIS HERITAGE SOFTAIL, CUSTOMIZED TO HIS OWN AUSSIE TASTE.

combat, numerous famous faces were riding other Harleys to help publicize the American company and, of course, themselves. Clark Gable was one such, riding his 1942 EL round Los Angeles, perfectly dressed in jacket, tie and hat, with a neat handkerchief sticking out of his breast pocket. He was apparently very fond of his 61cu in bike—at least he gave a damn about something.

Most bikers know that God rides a Harley-Davidson and of course the king did too. Numerous members of royalty have ridden Harley-Davidsons, from Viscount Linley in Britain to Crown Prince Olaf of Norway, but the king we're talking about here is of course Elvis Presley. As soon as he could get the money together from early recordings he went out and bought a KH 55cu in Harley. When the real

money started coming in he bought a new Sporster or big twin every year, normally picking it up from the factory himself.

The fresh-faced Elvis was a welcome boost to the Harley publicity machine, but if ever there was a cross-over between the media stars and the rough-living outlaws, it was Frenchman Serge Gainsbourg. He owned several big twins and was also close to Brigitte Bardot—you could really get to dislike the guy. She had her own bike, a 45cu in chopper, on which she memorably posed in her

BRITISH BOXER CHRIS EUBANK ON HIS
CUSTOMIZED FAT BOY WITH, FOR ONCE, HIS
TRADEMARK JODHPURS AND RIDING BOOTS NOT
LOOKING OUT OF PLACE.

MICKEY ROURKE SHOWS WHAT RIDING A
HARLEY-DAVIDSON CAN DO FOR YOUR HAIRSTYLE
IN THE FILM *HARLEY-DAVIDSON AND THE
MARLBORO MAN.*

 TOP

SYLVESTER STALLONE WITH ONE OF HIS HARLEYS, THIS TIME AN ELECTRA GLIDE BURIED UNDER THE CONTENTS OF A CUSTOM AND CHROME CATALOG.

own version of black leathers—mini-dress and thigh boots. She sang a song in 1966 stating that she didn't need anyone when she was on her Harley-Davidson, thus disappointing an entire generation of males. Serge Gainsbourg, though, the chain-smoking singer who always looked as if he needed some soap and sleep, was as fond of his own Harleys as he ever got about anything. Later in life he put a neat twist on the name with his track *Harley-David—Son Of A Bitch*.

Numerous other singers have followed in his footsteps, finding in the Harley-Davidson the perfect icon of rebellion. Everyone from Lou Reed through Billy Idol to Michael Hutchence have sprawled moodily for the photographer draped over various big V-twins. Presumably they have tried to ignore the fact that other singers have also owned

 LEFT

BILLY IDOL, AN ENGLISHMAN ABROAD, POSES BETWEEN INCIDENTS ON HIS HARLEY-DAVIDSON WIDE GLIDE. HE HAS CERTAINLY PUT THE MARQUE IN THE PAPERS.

FAT BOY AT THE LAUNCH OF PLANET HOLLYWOOD. NO, NOT HIM, THAT'S ARNIE SCHWARZENEGGER, THE MAN WHO MADE THE FAT BOY FAMOUS IN *TERMINATOR 2: JUDGMENT DAY*.

Harley-Davidsons, singers who might not quite add the necessary image of toughness. Singers like Neil Diamond and Olivia Newton-John.

The acting profession has displayed a similar split-personality approach to the whole subject. Those who spend a lot of time perfecting the tough-guy image, harking back to the days when 93% of all Harley owners were male, obviously have to have a Harley-Davidson, and roar around Hollywood. Mickey Rourke and Sylvester Stallone led the pack but Arnold Schwartenegger took the lead when he rode a Fat Boy in *Terminator 2: Judgment Day*, apparently pulling off some stunts it would be unwise for any owner to try to repeat.

SOME UNKNOWN PUBLICITY SEEKER TRIES TO GET HER PICTURE TAKEN BY THE SIMPLE EXPEDIENT OF STANDING NEXT TO A HARLEY-DAVIDSON SOFTAIL CUSTOM.

Not that Hollywood has the Harley-Davidson scene to itself. Harleys are far too trendy to be contained even in one continent, let alone one town. New York took the scene one stage further at the end of 1993 when the Harley-Davidson Café opened on the Avenue Of Americas. Some decades back this would have been a rough diner with "straights" made unwelcome, but times have changed. Now a diner with the Harley-Davidson name gets designed by an architect who normally designs top hotels in Hong Kong and Japan. The cuisine is called "Gourmet Road Food" but doesn't seem to include fresh road-kills. Needless to say, the restaurant is adorned with Harley-Davidsons, including the Captain America bike and a mannequin of Peter Fonda in *Easy Rider*. Committed bikers must be throwing up at the thought.

Even the outlaw biker is getting drawn in to an increasingly organized and acceptable set-up. In the 1960s, when dealers didn't even want to service the bikes of Hell's Angels and others, they

DANNII MINOGUE ON AN EVOLUTION MOTOR WITH A RETRO TREATMENT. IF SHE LASTS AS LONG AS THE HARLEY SHE'LL BE DOING WELL.

buy clothing from their own extensive range. What would Terry the Tramp have made of it all?

The point really is that, somehow, Harley-Davidsons have been expanding in all directions, moving up-market without losing a grip on the more realistic end of the sales graph. At the pinnacle, Harleys are ridden by some of the richest men in the world. People like Englishman Peter de Savary, who has hosted Harley-Davidson rallies at his Littlecote stately home. And people like the late Malcolm Forbes, a man who was so rich he had a magazine and listings named after him. He was an extremely serious fan and effective salesman for the Milwaukee iron. He used to tour around with like-minded employees and friends, a loose group known as "The Capitalist Tools." All riding Harleys in convoy, frequently riding under an immense hot-air balloon in, yes, the shape of a Harley-Davidson.

When he was friends with Elizabeth Taylor she came under the spell as well, and had her own Sportster, painted purple and with the logo of a perfume she was marketing. A purple Sportster with "Elizabeth Taylor's Passion" in gold scrollwork on the gas tank is a long way from what three men standing in a shed in 1903 would have had in mind. And yet it perfectly encapsulates what people have felt about their products ever since. The Japanese make technological marvels which you can like and admire, if not understand or work on, but a Harley-Davidson is a more personal affair between bike and rider. That is what Harley-Davidsons are all about—passion.

had to set up their own systems and servicing points. Their magazine, *Easyriders*, helped them with information and gave them a generous helping of good bikes and women whose clothes had mysteriously fallen off. By 1978 the factory and the publishing house had gone in such different directions that official Harley-Davidson advertising was pulled from a magazine that celebrated nothing but Harley-Davidsons. Things have now moved on to the point where *Easyriders* has opened gleaming showrooms and servicing outlets around America, where you can buy a used or custom Harley-Davidson, get something to eat or

WRESTLER HULK HOGAN TRIES TO GO FOR A RIDE WITHOUT CAUSING A FUSS. ARLEN NESS MADE HIM A HOG CALLED HULKSTER.